P9-CFF-374

Pizza Pie in the Sky

~ A Story About Illinois ~

Written by Karen Latchana Kenney

Illustrated by Bob Doucet

Consulting Editor, Diane Craig, M.A./Reading Specialist

Published by ABDO Publishing Company
8000 West 78th Street, Edina, Minnesota 55439.

Printed in the United States.

Editor: Pam Price
Content Developer: Nancy Tuminelly
Cover and Interior Design and Production:
Anders Hanson, Mighty Media
Photo Credits: Corbis Images, Fritz Geller-Grimm, iStockphoto (Jim Jurica, Eliza Snow), One Mile Up, James Gerholdt/Peter Arnold, Shutterstock, Quarter-dollar coin image from the United States Mint.

Library of Congress Cataloging-in-Publication Data

Kenney, Karen Latchana.
Pizza pie in the sky : a story about Illinois / Karen Latchana Kenney ; illustrated by Bob Doucet.
p. cm. -- (Fact & fable : state stories)
ISBN 978-1-60453-186-2
1. Illinois--Juvenile literature. I. Doucet, Bob, ill. II. Title.

F541.3.K46 2008
977.3--dc22

2008017873

Super SandCastle™ books are created by a team of professional educators, reading specialists, and content developers around five essential components—phonemic awareness, phonics, vocabulary, text comprehension, and fluency—to assist young readers as they develop reading skills and strategies and increase their general knowledge. All books are written, reviewed, and leveled for guided reading, early reading intervention, and Accelerated Reader® programs for use in shared, guided, and independent reading and writing activities to support a balanced approach to literacy instruction.

Table of Contents

painted turtle
(pg. 8)
Rockford
white oak tree
(pg. 4)
Chicago
Sears Tower
(pg. 9)
Moline
prairies
(pg. 12)
Peoria
Abraham Lincoln
statue (pg. 14)
Champaign
Quincy
Springfield
Route 66
road sign
(pg. 14)
ILLINOIS
US
66
Charleston
Mississippi River
PIZZA
THE SKY
ILLINOIS
Shawnee
National Forest
(pg. 19)
bluegills
(pg. 18)
Cairo
LEGEND
CAPITAL
STORY START
CITY
STORY PATH
RIVER
STORY END

White Oak

The Illinois state tree is the white oak. They can grow up to 100 feet (30.5 m) tall. They have light-colored bark on their trunks.

Pizza Pie in the Sky

Fall has come to Grayslake in Lake County, Illinois. The leaves of the white oak trees are turning red and purple. Misty, an orange, black, and white butterfly, holds on to a tree trunk and looks at the beautiful leaves.

Misty loves the colors in nature. The fall leaves dazzle her. Misty didn't notice that her friends were ready to leave. "Winter is coming. We've got to fly south, Misty!" George yelled. "Come on, we're going now!"

"I'll catch up in a minute," Misty shouted. The other monarch butterflies were already too far away to hear her.

Monarch Butterfly

The monarch butterfly is the Illinois state insect. Monarch butterflies travel about 3,000 miles (4,800 km) roundtrip every year. They spend the winter in the mountains of Mexico or California. They return north in the spring.

Violet

In 1907, schoolchildren voted to name the violet as the Illinois state flower. It has small blue flowers and dark green leaves.

Misty spotted some pretty blue flowers. She flew down for a closer look. After a while, she realized that her friends were gone. "Oh no!" Misty exclaimed, "George, where are you?" There was no answer. Misty was in trouble. She needed to fly south with George and the others. But she didn't know which way they went!

Misty took off to see if she could find the way south. Soon she saw what looked like an ocean. There was water as far as she could see. "This must be the great Lake Michigan that George told me about," she thought. Misty stopped at the shore for a drink of water. She wondered which way to fly to next.

Lake Michigan

Lake Michigan is one of the five Great Lakes. It forms the northeast border of Illinois. The Great Lakes are so large that you cannot see across them in most places. Lake Michigan is 118 miles (190 km) wide!

Painted Turtle

The painted turtle is the Illinois state reptile. They are colorful turtles that live in the water.

Sitting by the lake, Misty felt the cool, gentle wind blowing. Sunlight sparkled on the tips of the waves. She noticed a small head with two eyes floating in the water near the shore. The creature slowly rose out of the water and started coming toward her! It was a turtle with yellow marks on its face.

The turtle saw Misty and started to pull its head into its shell. "Wait!" Misty shouted. "I need your help!"

"What is it?" the turtle grumbled. "I'm in a hurry."

Misty said, "I'm trying to find my friends who are flying south."

The turtle answered, "I haven't seen your friends, but Chicago is south of here. Just keep the lake on your left." Misty thanked the turtle and headed off.

Chicago, Illinois

Chicago is the largest city in Illinois. It is known as the Windy City and is home to the Sears Tower. The Sears Tower is the tallest building in the United States.

Deep-Dish Pizza

Chicago is where deep-dish pizza was created. It is a very thick pizza. The sauce is often put on top of the other toppings.

After some time, Misty saw the tall buildings of Chicago along the lakeshore. She was hungry and lost. Misty landed outside a restaurant. The sign said Pizza Pie in the Sky. She tried the leftover pizza on a table. It was the best food she'd ever eaten! She ate so much that she had to rest before she could fly again.

A red bird landed next to Misty and chirped, "Hi, I'm Cal."

Chicago Deep-Dish Pizza

- 1 10-ounce can refrigerated pizza dough
- 2 cups chunky-style pizza or tomato sauce
- $1\frac{1}{2}$ cups shredded mozzarella cheese
- meat or vegetable toppings such as pepperoni slices, diced cooked chicken, sliced mushrooms, chopped onions, or black olives

Ask an adult to help cut and cook the food. Preheat the oven to 425°F (218°C). Grease a 13 × 9-inch (33 × 22-cm) pan with cooking spray or butter. Unroll the pizza dough and press it into the pan. Make sure the dough goes up the sides of the pan. Place the meat or vegetable toppings on the dough. Cover the toppings with mozzarella cheese. Finally, pour the sauce over the cheese. Bake the pizza for 20 minutes. Let the pizza cool for 5 minutes before cutting it.

Misty said, “I’m trying to follow my friends south. Have you seen a group of monarch butterflies?”

Cal replied, “No, I haven’t seen any butterflies. But the restaurant owner is flying his hot air balloon to Springfield. That’s south. You could ride along."

“Is he bringing more of this wonderful pizza?” asked Misty.

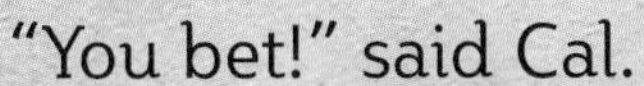

“You bet!” said Cal.

Cardinal

The cardinal is the Illinois state bird. This bird usually has red feathers. Some of them stick straight up from its head.

Prairie State

Illinois is known as the Prairie State. The official state prairie grass is big bluestem. The Indian Boundary Prairies are a group of four prairies south of Chicago. They cover over 300 acres (121.4 ha).

Misty landed on the basket just as the balloon took off. They rose high above Chicago. First they flew over the tall buildings. Then they passed houses. After the houses came farms and prairies. Misty happily ate more pizza while looking at the view below. The prairies stretched for miles in all directions. The prairie grasses rippled like waves in the wind.

The balloon landed in Springfield several hours later. Misty got off and tried to find someone to ask for directions. But everyone seemed to be too busy. Finally, she saw someone who wasn't moving at all. Maybe he would help her.

Springfield, Illinois

Springfield became the Illinois state capital in 1837. There were actually two other capital cities before Springfield. They were Kaskaskia and Vandalia.

Abraham Lincoln

Abraham Lincoln was the 16th president of the United States. He lived in Springfield, Illinois. There are many statues of Lincoln in the city of Springfield. Illinois is known as the Land of Lincoln.

As Misty moved closer, she saw a sign by the man's feet. It read Statue of Abraham Lincoln. "Oh!" Misty said to herself. "It's only a statue!" Suddenly a parade of old cars roared by. "What is going on?" Misty wondered out loud.

"It's the International Route 66 Mother Road Festival," piped up a voice. Misty looked all around and finally saw a little creature sitting on Lincoln's foot.

The creature looked like it was part frog and part snake. "I'm Sally the salamander!" the creature announced. "Are you new in town?"

Misty replied, "Yes, and I'm lost! I'm trying to find my friends. They are flying south."

Sally said, "These cars will be driving across Illinois on Route 66. You could follow them to the Mississippi River.

Eastern Tiger Salamander

The Illinois state amphibian is the eastern tiger salamander. It has yellow spots on its body, small eyes, and a rounded nose.

Lincoln Memorial Garden

Lincoln Memorial Garden is a 100-acre (40.5- ha) park and garden in Springfield, Illinois. It was created in 1936 and is home to many birds, wildflowers, insects, and turtles. Lake Springfield borders the Lincoln Memorial Garden.

Then turn left and follow the river south."

Misty thanked Sally for the advice and flew off after the parade of cars. Soon they passed a large garden. "Wow, the colors in that garden are beautiful!" Misty said to herself. "I'll just stop for a minute to get a closer look at those flowers."

She looked up just in time to see the last car drive out of sight. "Uh oh," she thought. "I'd better hurry and catch up!" Finally the cars and Misty came to the river that Sally had told her about. The parade of cars drove over the bridge. Misty turned left and followed the river.

Mississippi River

The Mississippi River is the western border of Illinois. It is the second-longest river in the United States. The Mississippi River runs from Minnesota to the Gulf of Mexico.

Bluegill

Bluegill is the Illinois state fish. Its name comes from the blue edging along its gills. Bluegills swim in groups of 20 to 30.

She looked down and saw a group of small fish in the river. They had bright blue edges on their gills. Misty was so busy looking at the fish that she almost flew straight into the water!

Then she saw a sign that read Shawnee National Forest. A familiar voice shouted, "Misty! Where have you been?" It was George!

"Oh, George, I wasn't paying attention and got lost!" Misty explained. "But I'm very glad that I got to see so much of Illinois. And I love deep-dish pizza! I can't wait to come back to Illinois in the spring!" Misty and her friends continued their flight south for the winter.

Shawnee National Forest

Shawnee National Forest is in the southern part of Illinois. It is the only national forest in Illinois. There are more than 500 kinds of animals, birds, and fish in this forest.

Illinois at a Glance

- **Abbreviation:** IL
- **Capital:** Springfield
- **Largest city:** Chicago (3rd-largest U.S. city)
- **Statehood:** December 3, 1818 (21st state)
- **Area:** 57,918 sq. mi. (150,009 sq km)
- **Nickname:** Prairie State
- **Motto:** State sovereignty, national union
- **State bird:** cardinal
- **State flower:** violet
- **State tree:** white oak
- **State mammal:** white-tailed deer
- **State insect:** monarch butterfly
- **State song:** "Illinois"

STATE SEAL

STATE FLAG

STATE QUARTER

The Illinois quarter portrays Abraham Lincoln, an outline of the state, a farm scene, and the Chicago skyline. The design symbolizes both the history and the future of Illinois.

What Do You Know?

How well do you remember the story? Match the pictures to the questions below! Then check your answers at the bottom of the page!

a. turtle

b. monarch butterfly

c. parade of cars

d. hot air balloon

e. Abraham Lincoln

f. bluegills

1. What kind of creature is Misty?
2. What kind of animal does Misty meet at Lake Michigan?
3. Whom does Misty see a statue of?
4. What does Misty ride to Springfield?
5. What does Misty follow to the river?
6. What does Misty see in the river?

Answers: 1|b 2|a 3|e 4|d 5|c 6|f

What to Do in Illinois

1 Go fly-fishing
Apple River Canyon State Park, Apple River

2 Meet Jane the dinosaur
Burpee Museum of Natural History, Rockford

3 Visit Navy Pier
Chicago

4 Take a paddleboat ride
Peoria RiverFront, Peoria

5 Visit a reindeer ranch
Hardy's Reindeer Ranch, Rantoul

6 Learn about the Amish
Illinois Amish Interpretive Center, Arcola

7 Visit a historic city
Cahokia Mounds, Collinsville

8 Explore a cave
Cave-in-Rock State Park, Cave-in-Rock